D1217051

^TE DUE

Pulleys

written by Caroline Rush
and
illustrated by Mike Gordon

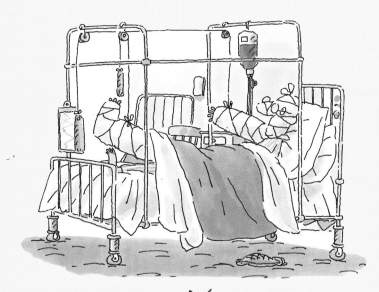

RSVP

RAINTREE
STECK-VAUGHN
PUBLISHERS
The Steck-Vaughn Company

Austin, Texas

Simple Science

Published by Raintree Steck-Vaughn Publishers, an imprint of Steck-Vaughn Company

Library of Congress Cataloging-in-Publication Data
Rush, Caroline.
Pulleys / written by Caroline Rush and illustrated by
    Mike Gordon.
        p.   cm.—(Simple science)
    Includes bibliographical references and index.
    Summary: An elementary introduction to how
    pulleys work.
    ISBN 0-8172-4503-0
    1. Pulleys—Juvenile literature.
    [1. Pulleys.]
    I. Gordon, Mike, ill. II. Title. III. Series:
    Simple science (Austin, Tex.)
    TJ1103.R76   1997
    621.8'11—dc20   96-22848

Printed in Italy and bound in the United States
1 2 3 4 5 6 7 8 9 0 0 01 00 99 98 97

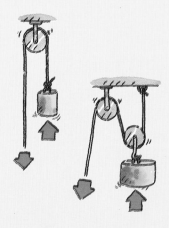

Contents

Our world would be a very different place without machines to help us.

A pulley is a simple lifting machine.

5

The idea for a pulley may have begun when someone threw a rope over a tree branch to help lift a heavy load.

That person discovered that it was easier to lift a heavy weight by pulling downward.

You attach one end of the rope to the object you want to lift and pass the rope around the groove of the wheel. When you pull the other end of the rope, you can raise the object.

8

 PULLEY WHEEL

 ROPE

Today's pulleys are made up of a wheel with a groove around the rim and a rope.

LOAD

EFFORT

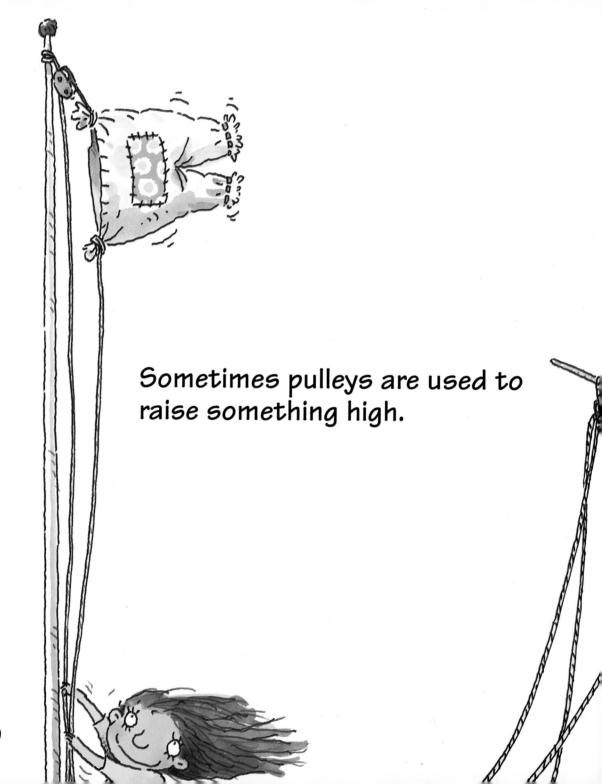

Sometimes pulleys are used to raise something high.

It is much easier to use a pulley than to climb up a flagpole and put the flag on top.

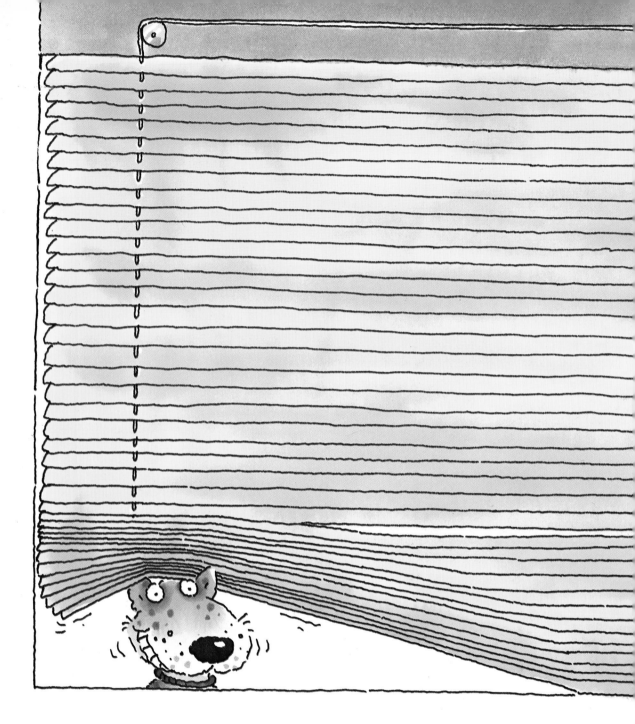

You use a pulley to raise a blind.

You may even be attached to a pulley in a hospital.

Pulleys are also used to lift heavy loads. It is easier to pull downward to lift a heavy weight because you can use your own body weight. Your body acts as a counterweight.

The more pulley wheels you use, the easier the job of lifting becomes. With two pulley wheels you can lift something twice as heavy as you can with one pulley wheel.

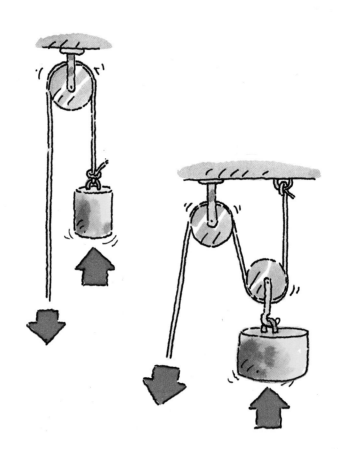

Experiment 1

Experiment 2

20

Three pulley wheels let you lift something three times as heavy.

Experiment 3

Cranes use lots of pulley wheels all together so they can lift really heavy loads from place to place.

23

When you ride in an elevator, a pulley is being used. The elevator is raised by strong cables around a pulley wheel.

An electric motor drives the pulley to raise the elevator.

25

Make your own pulley flagpole.

You will need:
2 plastic bottle tops
2 one-inch nails
12 inch length of wooden doweling
cereal box
glue
string
An adult to help you

1. Ask an adult to nail one bottle top to the top of the wooden doweling and one about 8 inches farther down. They must be loose enough to turn.

2. Turn the cereal box on its side and mark around the base of the doweling. Cut out the hole and slot your flagpole in its base. Decorate the base.

3. Cut out a paper flag and color it with your own design. Fold over one edge.

4. Lay your string along the fold with the center in the middle of the flag. Glue the edge down. Let dry.

5. Tie the string around the bottle tops so that it is quite tight. When you pull down on one side of the string, you will hoist your flag!

Glossary

Cable	A very strong rope, often made of metal.
Counter-weight	A weight used to pull down the end of a rope when an object is being lifted at the other end.
Crane	A large machine used for lifting very heavy objects.
Load	The weight of an object that is moved by a machine.
Pulley	A wheel with a rope around it used to lift an object up.
Rim	The outer edge of a wheel.

Suggestions for further activities

- Visit a building site and look at how pulleys are used there. See how pulleys lift building materials up scaffolding and how they are used within cranes.

- Experiment using different weights with a real pulley wheel. Can you add extra pulley wheels to enable you to lift heavier weights?

- Make a display of pictures from magazines or catalogs of different machines or pulleys that help them lift things up.

Books to read

Gordon, Mike and Maria. *Simple Science: Push and Pull*. New York: Thomson Learning, 1995.

Kerrod, Robin. *Force and Motion (Let's Investigate Science series)*. Bellmore, NY: Marshall Cavendish, 1994.

Murphy, Bryan. *Experiment with Movement*. Minneapolis: Lerner Publications, 1993.

Sauvain, Philip. *Motion (The Way It Works series)*. New York: New Discovery Books, 1992.

Williams, John. *Simple Science Projects with Machines*. Milwaukee: Gareth Stevens Inc., 1992.

For Older Readers

Macaulay, David. *The Way Things Work*. Boston: Houghton Mifflin, 1988.

Index